CW01512864

Original title:

Jasmine Twirls Within the Wizard Crib

Author: Sabrina Sarvik

ISBN HARDBACK: 978-1-80562-576-6

ISBN PAPERBACK: 978-1-80564-097-4

Fantasia in a Cradle of Light

In the twilight, whispers bloom,
Stars awaken, dispelling gloom.
A cradle forged in silken threads,
Where dreams take flight on silver beds.

Moonbeams dance on valleys wide,
Gentle secrets, the night will hide.
Listen close, the heart will see,
Fantasia sings in harmony.

A Weaver's Dreamscape

In threads of gold and starlit strands,
A weaver spins with delicate hands.
Each pattern tells a tale anew,
Of worlds unseen and wonders true.

Night's tapestry, rich and deep,
Holds the dreams that we all keep.
In vibrant hues, our hopes alight,
A dreamscape spun from pure delight.

The Floating Garden of Echoes

A garden floats on gentle streams,
Where echoes weave through starlit dreams.
Petals whisper soft and low,
In twilight breezes, secrets flow.

Each flower sways with timeless grace,
Reflecting the moon's silver face.
In this haven of peace and light,
Echoes linger, taking flight.

Rituals of the Celestial Blossom

Underneath the ancient skies,
Celestial blossoms bid their sighs.
In rituals of night and day,
They twirl in magic's vibrant play.

A gentle glow, the stars align,
With every petal, love divine.
Through cosmic paths, their secrets share,
In whispered prayers, we feel their care.

The Child and the Enchantment of Blooms

In a garden where dreams softly dance,
A child spins tales of magic and chance.
With flowers that whisper their secrets so deep,
Each petal a promise, each blossom a leap.

Beneath the bright canopy of azure sky,
Curious creatures join in, oh my!
With laughter that lilts on a breeze that flows,
Together they weave where the wild magic grows.

A butterfly flutters, a dragonfly twirls,
In this world of wonder, each moment unfurls.
The child dreams of kingdoms where wishes come true,
Among blooms of all colors, in radiant hues.

As twilight descends, a soft glow appears,
The moon whispers wisdom, dissolving all fears.
In the heart's quiet chambers, with stars overhead,
The child finds a path where their spirit is led.

So, remember this tale when the dark night calls,
Of a child and enchantments in bloom's gentle thralls.
In gardens of hope, let your own stories zoom,
For magic awaits, in the heart of each bloom.

Mystical Fragrance of Starlit Stories

Underneath the vast canvas, a quilt of the night,
Stars twinkle softly, a shimmering sight.
Each flicker a story, woven with care,
In the dance of the cosmos, dreams linger in air.

A gentle breeze carries the tales of the skies,
Of worlds yet discovered, where mystery lies.
The fragrance of starlight, so sweet and so rare,
Wrapped in the whispers, a celestial share.

With each tiny beacon, a wish is bestowed,
A map of adventures in silver threads flowed.
The constellations beckon, both daring and bold,
To wander through spaces where legends unfold.

A child gazes upward, imagination alight,
With dreams of enchantment that shimmer at night.
They trace the formations with fingers of hope,
In the wonders of starlight, their spirit can cope.

As dawn greets the sky with its luminous hue,
The stories may fade, yet still feel so true.
In the heart of a dreamer, in shadows and glow,
The fragrance of starlit tales continues to flow.

The Illusion of Wandering Petals

In whispers soft the petals drift,
They float with grace, a magic gift.
Each flutter speaks of secrets old,
Of stories wrapped in twilight's hold.

Beneath the stars, they dance and sway,
In moonlit dreams, they often play.
A tapestry of colors bright,
They weave the fabric of the night.

In gardens lush, where shadows creep,
The petals whisper, secrets keep.
Their fragrance lingers, sweet and rare,
A fragrant sigh upon the air.

Through winding paths, they softly glide,
A gentle breeze, their only guide.
With every turn, a tale revives,
The essence of their dance survives.

For in the night, where magic brews,
The wandering petals sing their hues.
A fleeting glance, a wistful glance,
In nature's waltz, we find our chance.

Mantra of the Mystic Gardens

In gardens where the moonlight glows,
A mantra hums, a secret flows.
Each flower speaks a timeless tune,
Beneath the watchful eye of noon.

The ancient trees, with branches wide,
Guard whispered truths, where dreams abide.
Their roots entwined in sacred soil,
A testament to nature's toil.

With every bloom, a voice is heard,
In rustling leaves, a magic word.
The paths invite us, step by step,
Through realms where mystery is kept.

Amidst the blooms in vibrant hue,
The spirits dance, both old and new.
In fragrant air, the memories rise,
In secret places, laughter lies.

So wander here, in twilight's grace,
And find your name in nature's embrace.
The mantra lingers, soft and clear,
A symphony for all who hear.

Whirling Colors in the Midnight Air

Amidst the night, where shadows blend,
Whirling colors twist and bend.
A canvas painted deep and wide,
With every hue, the stars confide.

The midnight air, a breath of dreams,
In vibrant whispers, magic streams.
With every twirl, a splash of light,
Illuminating the whispering night.

Under the gaze of a silvery moon,
Dance the colors, a soft, sweet tune.
In spirals bright, the cosmos sings,
To celebrate the joy it brings.

The dark might hide what light reveals,
In joyful swirls, the heart reveals.
An endless dance, a swirling flare,
Awash with wonder, everywhere.

As night unfolds its mystic spell,
In colors bright, all tales will dwell.
The whirling twirls of magic rare,
Embrace the world, suspend all care.

Blossoms in a Dream Weaver's Embrace

In twilight's grasp, where dreams are spun,
Blossoms rest as day is done.
Each petal cradled, soft and light,
In silver shadows kissing night.

The dream weaver with gentle hands,
Weaves tales of love in silken strands.
Each blossom glows with stories true,
In whispered hopes, their colors grew.

As moonbeams dance in tender grace,
The blossoms sway, a sweet embrace.
In fragrant air, their voices blend,
A lullaby that will not end.

With every breeze that stirs the night,
The blossoms twirl in pure delight.
In nature's cradle, softly laid,
The dreams are born, the fears allayed.

So linger here, where wonders bloom,
In every corner, dispel the gloom.
In dream weaver's arms, we find our place,
Embraced by blossoms, kissed by grace.

Nighttime Tales of Fragrant Enchantment

In the hush of the night sky, softly they sway,
Moonlit whispers dance, casting shadows at play.
Beneath silver stars, secrets unfold,
Fragrant tales of enchantment, waiting to be told.

Petals of twilight, shimmering bright,
Lend their sweet perfume to the canvas of night.
Dreamers wander through the fragrant embrace,
In gardens of wonder, they find their place.

Ancient trees hum a lullaby low,
While the fireflies weave a soft, glowing show.
Every breath captured, like a wish set free,
In nighttime's enchantment, just let it be.

So linger a moment, let the magic arise,
Underneath the vast and twinkling skies.
For night carries stories, enchanting and deep,
In the heart of the world, where dreams gently sleep.

The Cosmic Embrace of Petals

Petals drift softly, like whispers of dreams,
Carried by starlight, on moonlit streams.
In gardens celestial, they dance and they twirl,
A tapestry woven in a cosmic swirl.

Bright blooms of color, a galaxy's call,
Kissing the heavens, where soft shadows fall.
Each fragrance a wish, a story untold,
A moment of magic, in colors so bold.

With every petal that flutters and flies,
Whispers of wonder escape to the skies.
The cosmos rejoices in fragrant delight,
In the embrace of petals, all things feel right.

So gather the stardust, breathe deep in the air,
For the beauty of blossoms is beyond compare.
In this cosmic embrace, our spirits unite,
Like stars in the darkness, we shimmer, we light.

Dreaming in a Mystic Garden

In a garden enchanted, where magic does bloom,
The air thick with dreams, like a sweet silver plume.
Where whispers of fairies weave tales in the shade,
And each petal unfurls a secret cascade.

Dewdrops glisten softly, like jewels on the leaves,
As nightingales serenade, the heart gently cleaves.
In shadows of twilight, with starlight aglow,
Nature spins stories, with wisdom to show.

With every soft breeze, the flowers awake,
In colors of twilight, their beauty we take.
The moon drapes her veil, as silence descends,
In this mystic haven, where dreaming transcends.

To wander in wonder, amongst blossoms of light,
Is to capture the essence of pure, sweet delight.
In the heart of this garden, where secrets are spun,
We whisper our wishes; our dreaming's begun.

Secrets of the Twirling Flora

In the heart of the forest, where shadows do play,
The twirling flora dance in a magical way.
Each blossom a dancer, with colors so rare,
Whispering secrets in the crisp evening air.

Leaves rustle softly, a gentle embrace,
As flowers spin tales in their delicate grace.
Through twilight they weave, with laughter and cheer,
A symphony framed in the world we hold dear.

With every soft waltz, new stories unfold,
Adventures of nature, both tender and bold.
For the flora keep secrets, in petals and bark,
With every twirl and flutter, they dance in the dark.

So listen intently, hear the rustling sound,
For the secrets of flora in whispers abound.
In the rhythm of nature, a timeless embrace,
Twirling together in this sacred space.

Beyond the Veil of Petals

In gardens where secrets softly dwell,
The petals whisper tales they tell.
Beneath the stars, in twilight's glow,
Lies a world where dreams do flow.

With every breeze, a spell is cast,
Ancient echoes of the past.
Through veils of color, spirits glide,
In the heart of nature, magic hides.

Each flower holds a sacred thought,
Of love and loss, of battles fought.
Beyond the veil, the truth awaits,
In every blossom, destiny creates.

In moonlit nights, where shadows dance,
The petals weave a tender trance.
A journey waits for those who dare,
To lift the veil and breathe the air.

So wander forth, O seeker true,
In fields of dreams, chase what is due.
Emerge from shadows, find the light,
Beyond the veil, embrace the night.

The Melody of Wandering Blooms

Where wildflowers sway in sweet delight,
The melody shimmers, a joyous flight.
Each blossom's laugh, a vibrant tune,
Dancing softly to the croon.

The rustling leaves, a gentle choir,
Lift the heart like a soaring fire.
In fields of gold, their voices rise,
Underneath the endless skies.

Voices of petals, a vibrant spell,
In every corner, magic dwells.
With colors bright, they sing of peace,
A harmony that will never cease.

The breeze carries whispers far and wide,
Of love and laughter, it won't hide.
In this symphony of nature's grace,
Find the rhythm, lose the race.

So walk with me, where blooms reside,
In every step, let joy abide.
The melody plays, a sweet embrace,
In wandering blooms, we find our place.

When Magic Meets the Moon

When twilight falls and shadows creep,
The moon awakens, secrets keep.
A silver glow on nightly shores,
Where magic swells and mystery soars.

In the stillness, the air ignites,
With whispers soft, enchanting sights.
Stars unveil their tales of old,
In lunar light, the brave are bold.

The world transforms in moonlight's beam,
Where wishes dance and stardust gleam.
A crescent smile from skies above,
Awakens hearts to dreams of love.

With every glance upon the night,
The magic whispers, a pure delight.
As shadows blend with dreams undone,
When magic meets the moon, we're one.

So linger longer in this glow,
Let wonders grow and rivers flow.
Embrace the night, let spirits rise,
For when the moon shines, magic lies.

Serendipity in the Garden of Night

In gardens cloaked in softest night,
Where stars sprinkle dreams, pure delight.
Serendipity paints the skies,
A tapestry where chance defies.

Beneath the boughs, the secrets twine,
In every shadow, magic shines.
The flowers bloom with gentle grace,
Unraveling stories time can trace.

In whispers low, the night unfolds,
As every petal, a tale it holds.
With fragrance sweet, the air enchants,
Inviting hearts to dream and dance.

With every step, serendipity calls,
In this garden, where nightly falls.
Lost in wonder, find your way,
In the embrace of night's soft sway.

So take a breath in this sacred space,
Let fortune guide you, find your place.
For in the dark, with stars so bright,
Serendipity reigns in the garden of night.

Enchanted Petals Dance

In the glade where shadows play,
Petals twirl and softly sway,
Magic lurks in twilight's grace,
Whispers float in nature's embrace.

Dewdrops glisten on soft blooms,
Catching light in vibrant rooms,
Colors bright in moonlight's gleam,
Nature sings a sweetened dream.

Gentle breezes weave around,
Carrying the sweetest sound,
Of laughter shared beneath the trees,
As petals dance upon the breeze.

In this realm of pure delight,
Hope unfurls beneath the night,
Every flower, every glance,
Is woven deep in magic's dance.

So come and join this night-time song,
Where all the weary souls belong,
In the garden's secret trance,
Where we all can dream and prance.

Starlit Whispers in the Nursery

In the stillness of the night,
Stars above burn oh so bright,
Softly humming lullabies,
Carried on the moonlit sighs.

Tiny hands and sleepy eyes,
Underneath the velvet skies,
Fairy tales weave through the air,
Filling hearts with magic's care.

Cradled dreams on silver beams,
Dance in dew, a blur of dreams,
As shadows play on nursery walls,
And mother softy calls.

With each star a wish unfurls,
Whispered hopes of boys and girls,
Woven in the night's embrace,
In this gentle, sacred space.

So rest now, my dear little one,
The world outside has just begun,
With starlit whispers softly spun,
In dreams, adventures now run.

The Sorcerer's Lullaby

Close your eyes, the night is still,
The world sleeps while magic spills,
Ancient words in softest sighs,
Float like stars across the skies.

In shadows deep where secrets lie,
A sorcerer sings a lullaby,
Enchanting notes that gently weave,
A tapestry of dreams to leave.

With each breath, the candles glow,
Casting warmth in softened flow,
Let their light guide you to sleep,
In realms of wonder – safe and deep.

Echoes of the spells long cast,
Whispers of the shrouded past,
Laden with both hope and fear,
Yet in slumber, all is clear.

So drift away on twilight's breeze,
With thoughts of magic and the trees,
For in the depth of slumber's sigh,
The heart will dance – with dreams that fly.

Garden Dreams Under Moonlight

In the garden, blooms align,
Underneath the silver line,
Where wishes gather, hopes ignite,
And softly hum beneath the night.

Petals glimmer, dew drops shine,
In every corner, magic twines,
While shadows sway and breezes play,
In dreams that dance, they twirl away.

Whispers of the night entwine,
With laughter that the stars define,
Every flower, every brush,
Leads to dreams, a gentle hush.

Where moonlight drips upon the grass,
And time seems still as minutes pass,
In this haven, hearts take flight,
Lost in love beneath the night.

So linger long in whispered glee,
In this garden, wild and free,
For dreams are born where hearts align,
Under the spell of moonlit shine.

Moonlit Dreams on Velvet Screams

In shadows cast by silver light,
The whispering trees sway through the night.
Dreams woven soft in moon's embrace,
A dance of secrets, leaving no trace.

Velvet screams echo deep within,
A tale of lost where stars begin.
The nightingale's song, a haunting tune,
Guided by the glow of a wistful moon.

Through misty paths, the twilight glows,
Veils of magic the darkness shows.
In every rustle and every sigh,
The world transforms, and soars on high.

As shadows blend with twilight's cheer,
Whimsical dreams, they linger near.
In pockets of night where wonders dwell,
The heart can tell its own sweet spell.

With every breath, the fabric weaves,
A tapestry of hopes and leaves.
In moonlit dreams where fantasies beam,
Awake your soul; it's time to dream.

A Sorceress Rests in the Flora

In a glade where wildflowers grow,
A sorceress rests, her powers aglow.
With petals soft, she weaves her spell,
Amongst the blooms, her magic dwells.

Her fingers dance on silken bloom,
Awakening life with a gentle tune.
The forest whispers ancient lore,
As she conjures dreams to explore.

Beneath the canopy, shadows twine,
In every leaf, her secrets shine.
With eyes like starlight, deep and wise,
She sees the truth that never dies.

In twilight's arms, the world transforms,
Amidst the whispers, the magic warms.
A guardian of spirits, she calls their names,
In this enchanted realm where beauty reigns.

So, linger long, where shadows grow,
In the sorceress's heart, let your spirit flow.
Among the flora, find your kin,
For in the wild, the magic begins.

Enchantment in a Twisting Breeze

Through fields of dreams, the breezes play,
Carrying whispers of night and day.
A dance of leaves in the shimmering light,
As hearts awaken to the summer night.

With every twist, the magic swirls,
An ancient song as the daylight twirls.
In every gust, a story flows,
Of lost realms where enchantment grows.

The petals flutter, a soft ballet,
In the gentle breeze, they find their way.
With laughter echoed and shadows cast,
Each moment cherished, each memory vast.

As twilight deepens with stars so bright,
The air hums softly, a pure delight.
In the tapestry of the evening's sigh,
The world unveils its secrets shy.

So chase the breezes, let spirits soar,
For magic lives in the tales of yore.
In every whisper and guiding breeze,
Find the enchantment that aims to please.

Magic Unfolds Among Petal Threads

In gardens lush where colors blend,
Magic unfolds, the start and end.
With petal threads, they weave their tale,
A fragrant dream on a silken gale.

In every bloom, a story sings,
Of captivating worlds and wondrous things.
The honeyed scent, a siren's call,
Where hearts unite and shadows fall.

As sunlight kisses the morning dew,
Each drop reflects the skies so blue.
In laughter's echo and shadows cast,
Find a magic that forever lasts.

Through winding paths of nature's grace,
Every turn reveals a sacred space.
With enchanted whispers, the breezes play,
Awakening moods at the break of day.

So linger here, where petals bloom,
In the magic's heart, let love consume.
For among these threads, the dreams conspire,
To stir the soul and set it afire.

The Cradle of Ethereal Petals

In twilight's hush, the petals sway,
Soft whisper secrets in soft array.
Cradled in dew, they shimmer bright,
A dance of dreams in the fading light.

Beneath the stars, the blossoms breathe,
Magical tales in the moonlight sheathe.
Gentle caress of a breeze so light,
Lullabies weaving through lover's night.

Petals unfurl with a tender grace,
In their embrace, a dreamy place.
Each hue a story, a hidden song,
In the cradle where hearts belong.

Night's velvet cloak, a soft embrace,
Within this realm, all fears erase.
Whispers of hope in the fragrant air,
In this cradle, we find our care.

So linger here as the shadows play,
In the cradle of petals, we'll stay.
With stardust prayers and wishes anew,
In every bloom, my heart finds you.

Dancing Light on Delicate Leaves

Beneath the canopy, sunlight weaves,
A tapestry bright on delicate leaves.
Each fluttering ray a fleeting kiss,
In nature's sway, we find our bliss.

Whispers of breezes tickle the air,
As shadows play without a care.
In the dance of light, a world unfolds,
Stories of magic in colors bold.

Glistening drops from last night's rain,
Anointed jewels that shimmer and gain.
Each leaf a canvas for sunlight's art,
A symphony of nature, a work of heart.

Amidst this wonder, we find reprieve,
In the quiet moments, our spirits believe.
To dance with light, oh how sweet the chase,
In delicate leaves, we find our place.

So let us wander 'neath branches wide,
With laughter and dreams, side by side.
For time is but a fleeting thief,
In the dance of light, we'll find our belief.

Echoes of Enchantment at Dusk

When dusk descends with a gentle sigh,
Echoes of magic linger nearby.
The world holds its breath, in soft repose,
Where secrets linger and twilight glows.

In rustling leaves, the stories sigh,
Of ancient spells and time gone by.
Shadows stretch with an elegant grace,
Enchanted whispers in twilight's embrace.

As stars awaken, a shimmering choir,
Voices of starlight, a soft desire.
In every flicker, a tale is spun,
A dance of dreams, where all things run.

The nightingale sings of what's yet to be,
In the arms of dusk, we're wild and free.
With each hushed note, the heart takes flight,
In echoes of enchantment, love ignites.

So linger a moment in this sacred space,
Where dreams take shape and time leaves a trace.
In the dusk's embrace, hear the heart's call,
For echoes of enchantment will beckon us all.

Celestial Revels in the Flowerbed

Amidst the blooms where the wild things grow,
Celestial revels in a vibrant show.
Petals adorned in the night's soft veil,
Each fragrance whispers a story to tell.

The moon spills silver on blossoms bright,
As stars bear witness to the joy of night.
In the flowerbed, a hidden delight,
Where dreams are woven with threads of light.

In laughter, blooms sway to a tune,
A symphony offered by the night's sweet moon.
Each blossom twirls in a cosmic dance,
Through glimmers and shadows, lost in a trance.

Hearts entwined in the fragrant air,
With every heartbeat, we share and dare.
In the flowerbed's warmth, we lay our heads,
Beneath the celestial canvas, love spreads.

So join the revels, let spirits soar,
In nature's embrace, we'll seek for more.
For in this garden, time does suspend,
In celestial revels, love knows no end.

Silken Threads of Magic

In the quiet glens where whispers weave,
Dreams are spun on a silken sleeve.
Glimmers of hope in the twilight gleam,
Woven together in a tender dream.

Each thread a tale of the night's embrace,
A dance that hides in an endless space.
Mystic lights wrap the world in gold,
Secrets of magic quietly told.

Gentle winds carry soft-spoken lore,
With every step, we unlock the door.
At the edge of dusk, where shadows twirl,
We discover the wonders that gently unfurl.

Stars overhead in the velvet sky,
Whisper their secrets as the night drifts by.
A tapestry stitched by the moonlight's hand,
Threads of enchantment across the land.

So let your heart dance to the ethereal song,
In the embrace of magic, where you belong.
With every breath, let the stories glean,
In silken threads, we find what's unseen.

Spells and Shadows in Bloom

In twilight gardens, shadows cast,
Where spells awaken, mysteries vast.
Petals whisper of ancient lore,
A symphony sung from the forest floor.

Among the thorns, the secrets hide,
With each soft breeze, they stir inside.
A flicker of light where no man treads,
The dance of magic where hope spreads.

Beneath the stars, enchantments grow,
In the heart of night, they softly glow.
With every breath of the cool night air,
The world is woven with magic rare.

Charming notes from a spellbound flute,
Rustle of leaves where dreams take root.
In gardens deep, where shadows loom,
The heart beats true, Spells in bloom.

Follow the path where the wild things roam,
In shadows' embrace, we find our home.
Together we'll weave the starlight bright,
In a dance of magic, through the night.

A Blossom's Secret Waltz

Under a canopy of twilight gray,
A blossom sways in a secret ballet.
Glistening dew upon silken leaves,
Whispers of twilight, the heart believes.

Dancing softly on the evening breeze,
In petals' lull, the world finds ease.
A hidden waltz, serene and sweet,
Where earth and sky in harmony meet.

Moonlight spills in a silver stream,
Awakening dreams from a gentle dream.
In fragrant whispers, the night unfolds,
The story of magic through petals told.

Through dusk-lit paths where time stands still,
The blossoms twirl with a graceful thrill.
Each twirling leaf a soft-spoken vow,
In the soft caress of the night, here and now.

So let us dance beneath the stars,
With open hearts and guiding scars.
In every step, a story enchants,
A blossom's secret in midnight's dance.

The Mysterious Blooming

In the heart of the forest, a whisper grows,
A tale of the magic in every rose.
Beneath the shadows where secrets cling,
The night breathes softly, awakening spring.

With petals closed in a slumber deep,
The world holds its breath, in silence we keep.
A stirring of life in the moon's embrace,
A mystical blooming in hidden space.

Twilight hues paint the sky anew,
Inviting the magic in every view.
With every blossom, a promise unfolds,
In the cool night air, a story behold.

The fragrance drifts on the velvet air,
A question posed in the night's fair.
What mysteries lay in a single bloom?
A touch of wonder, dispelling gloom.

So linger a moment, let the magic in,
With each secret shared, true life begins.
In the dance of the night, let the blossoms sing,
For the mysterious blooming, magic we bring.

Moonlit Revelries in the Enchanted Grove

Beneath the moon's soft silver glow,
Whispers weave where wildflowers grow.
Dancing shadows, a secret throng,
In the grove, where dreams belong.

Stars flicker in a velvet sky,
Time slips by with a gentle sigh.
The nightingale sings a lonesome tune,
While magic swirls like petals strewn.

Mirthful pixies flit and play,
Casting spells in the milky gray.
Laughter echoes through ancient trees,
Carried forth on the evening breeze.

Crickets chirp their midnight hymn,
A dance of shadows, the lights grow dim.
In this realm where the wild things roam,
Hearts find solace, and spirits come home.

When dawn's first light begins to break,
The grove awakens from its slumber quake.
Yet memories linger, sweetly spun,
In this enchanted place where night was fun.

A Voyage Through Floral Fantasies

In gardens rich with colors bright,
Where every petal holds a light.
We sail on dreams, on fragrant streams,
Through floral realms where magic gleams.

Butterflies dance, on currents soft,
Playful whispers rise aloft.
Sunlight trickles in golden rays,
Illuminating hidden ways.

The roses hum a timeless tune,
While daisies sway with the afternoon.
Tulips bow in a gentle breeze,
As nature pours her heart with ease.

Petal boats on a crystal lake,
Float on wishes, dreams to make.
Lavender fields stretch far and wide,
A canvas painted, nowhere to hide.

In this realm where whispers blend,
Floral fantasies never end.
We journey forth with hearts ablaze,
In the garden's tender, endless maze.

The Call of the Cosmic Blossom

In a universe where stardust sings,
A blossom blooms with cosmic wings.
It calls to hearts from worlds afar,
Guiding seekers to the stars.

A kaleidoscope of colors bright,
In every hue, an ancient light.
It twirls and sways in galactic dance,
A wondrous tale of fate and chance.

The petals hold wisdom, secrets deep,
In their embrace, the cosmos weeps.
With every breath, it spins and twirls,
Awakening dreams in a thousand worlds.

As comets blaze and meteors fall,
The cosmic blossom hears the call.
With open hearts, we reach and soar,
To grasp the magic, forevermore.

In the silence of the twilight glow,
We find the path where dreams can flow.
The cosmic dance of life unfolds,
In the bloom of stars, our story holds.

Enchanted Reveries in a Child's Heart

In lands where innocence takes flight,
A child's heart glows with purest light.
Each dream ignites a world anew,
With every laugh, the wonder grew.

The trees speak softly, secrets shared,
With gentle whispers, they have cared.
In the meadows, games of hide-and-seek,
Where magic sparkles, and voices speak.

Clouds transform in a sky so blue,
Into castles where dreams come true.
With crayons drawn on tabletops,
Imagination never stops.

At twilight's touch, the stars awake,
With every twinkling, promises make.
In sleepy tales, adventures weave,
A tapestry of joy to believe.

In a child's heart, the world unfolds,
With enchanted reveries, dreams untold.
As night embraces, softly and sweet,
In every heartbeat, the magic's complete.

The Garden Where Shadows Play

In a garden where shadows play,
Whispers dance both night and day,
Petals flutter, secrets hum,
Beneath the moon, the fairies drum.

Glimmers of light on leaf and vine,
Magic sparkles, soft and fine,
With every step, enchantments weave,
In the hush, the heart believes.

Trees entwined in shadows cold,
Stories of love and courage told,
Gentle breezes carry dreams,
In this realm of silver gleams.

Butterflies flit, in colors bright,
Guiding wanderers through the night,
Nature's song, a soothing balm,
In this place, the world feels calm.

So linger here, where shadows play,
Embrace the magic, let it stay,
In the garden, where hearts renew,
You'll find the wonders meant for you.

Spellbound in a Fragrant Realm

In a realm where the blossoms sigh,
Fragrant tales drift and fly,
Each petal holds a whispered word,
Spellbound by the dreams unheard.

Lavender sways in the gentle breeze,
Carrying secrets with such ease,
A dance of colors, sweet and bright,
Crafting magic in the soft twilight.

Honeyed aromas wrap around,
In every corner, enchantment found,
Glimmers of hope in evening's glow,
As the moon sets the flowers aglow.

Birds of song serenade the stars,
Sharing light from Venus and Mars,
With every breath, the heart entwines,
In this fragrant realm, love shines.

So wander deep, let your spirit soar,
In the magic that awakens more,
With every step, you sense the charms,
In this spellbound land of arms.

Enchanted Vines and Secrets Sweet

Amidst the enchanted vines so rare,
Lies a world beyond compare,
With every twist, a story waits,
Guarded by time, behind the gates.

Sunlight dances through the leaves,
Whispering tales that nature weaves,
Secrets sweet as summer's breath,
Life and magic, blended with death.

Beneath the boughs, the shadows play,
In the thickets, fairies sway,
With fingers green, they cradle dreams,
In the silence, hope redeems.

Nature's art on canvas bright,
Unfurling wonders in the night,
Each enchanted vine a thread,
Binding tales of love long spread.

So tread softly, and heed the call,
Of the secrets held within the wall,
For in this verdant, lush retreat,
Magic and heart forever meet.

The Sorceress of Soft Night Blossoms

In shadows deep, where wishes grow,
Dwells a sorceress, calm and low,
With soft night blossoms in her hair,
She weaves her dreams with tender care.

Moonlit paths where roses bloom,
Her laughter chases away the gloom,
With every step, new magic brews,
In this realm of midnight hues.

Her fingers trace the stars above,
Sending whispers of peace and love,
In her presence, the world feels right,
A gentle guide through the soft night.

Beneath the sky, where hopes take flight,
She dances under the silver light,
With petals soft, she graces the air,
A sorceress beyond compare.

So seek her out on twilight's breeze,
With open heart, your worries seize,
For in her gentle, glowing light,
All is possible in the night.

Harmonies in the Dreaming Garden

In the garden where secrets bloom,
Whispers weave through the fragrant gloom.
Colorful petals in silence sway,
As twilight deepens and night holds sway.

Moonlit shadows dance on the stone,
Gentle breezes in soft tones moan.
Each flower sings a tale so sweet,
A symphony where magic and nature meet.

Stars align with a twinkling grace,
In the heart of this enchanted space.
Bumblebees hum their dulcet tune,
Inviting dreams beneath the moon.

The willow weeps with a tender sigh,
As dreams take flight into the sky.
Each note a flutter, pure and clear,
In this magical garden, we hold dear.

With every breath, the night unfolds,
A tapestry of stories told.
In the dreaming garden, we find our place,
Where harmonies linger in soft embrace.

Whimsical Whispers Underneath the Sky

Underneath the ever-changing skies,
Whispers float where the wild birds fly.
Starlight dances on the silver streams,
Mirroring the colors of our dreams.

Clouds gather with tales of old,
Kissing the earth with a touch of gold.
In the embrace of the midnight air,
We find secrets hidden everywhere.

The moon grins down with a playful glance,
Inviting all to a starry dance.
With laughter that tickles the balmy breeze,
Whimsical whispers weave through the trees.

Every leaf rustles with a song,
Echoing tales of where we belong.
Even the shadows of the night,
Hold stories waiting to take flight.

As dreams swirl in the cool night mist,
We treasure moments that none could resist.
In this world where magic flows so high,
We revel in whimsical whispers and sigh.

The Enchanted Flora's Reverie

In a realm where the flowers gleam,
Lies a garden steeped in a gentle dream.
Each bloom a secret, a whispered thought,
In the dance of petals, enchantment is sought.

Sunrise casts a gold-hued glow,
Awakening flora in a soft tableau.
Butterflies brush on silken air,
Painting stories only the brave would dare.

Petals flutter with voices bright,
Singing songs that ignite the night.
Glistening dew like stars aglow,
As day surrenders to twilight's flow.

The lilting breeze carries a melody,
From blossoms swaying in symphony.
Nature's magic, a tranquil sound,
In the enchanted flora, peace is found.

As dusk embraces the garden fair,
Whispers of wonder fill the air.
Let us linger where dreams are spun,
In the reverie of blossoms, one by one.

A Dance of Petals in the Night

When twilight wraps the world in lace,
A dance of petals begins to trace.
In the hush where wonders stir,
Gentle breezes begin to purr.

Birds hush their songs, in shadows hide,
While moonbeams touch the forest wide.
Whispers twirl with the softest grace,
Inviting all to this magical place.

Each petal sways, a dancer fair,
With fragrant scents that fill the air.
In their movement, the night's delight,
Weaves a tapestry of sheer moonlight.

Starlit eyes glance down with glee,
As nature twirls in harmony.
Among the blooms, we find our way,
In the petal's dance, we lose the fray.

As dreams awaken with softest sighs,
We join the waltz 'neath the starry skies.
In this nocturnal splendor so right,
We are swept in a dance of petals tonight.

Whispers of Enchanted Blooms

In a glade where lilies sigh,
And moonlight drapes the trees,
Whispers rise like gentle ties,
Dancing on the evening breeze.

Petals soft as secret dreams,
Glisten in the twilight's glow,
They reveal the latent schemes,
Of realms where only magic flows.

Bumblebees with tales to tell,
Flit beneath the hanging vines,
In the air, a distant bell,
Strikes a note of ancient signs.

Violets wink in playful jest,
As shadows gather close and near,
In their clasp, a hidden quest,
Urging hearts to shed their fear.

Underneath the starlit dome,
The blooms sing of love's embrace,
In this garden, all can roam,
Finding joy in magic's grace.

Spells in the Garden's Embrace

In the garden where herbs entwine,
Whispers float on petals light,
Chanting softly, line by line,
Crafting spells in the hush of night.

Beneath the arching willow veil,
Fingers weave a storied thread,
Casting dreams upon the trail,
Where every thought and wish is spread.

Roses blush with secrets bold,
Each thorn hides a tale of yore,
In their beauty, legends told,
Guarding hearts forevermore.

Under the moon's watchful eye,
Charmed with visions soft and sweet,
Starlit paths and clouds awry,
Lead the lost to fate's heartbeat.

In this haven, life resumes,
Where every whisper holds a key,
Unlocking nature's vibrant blooms,
Binding spirits wild and free.

The Dancer and the Sorcerer's Lair

In the shadows of the night,
A dancer swirls with grace,
Her heart aglow, a beacon bright,
Chasing dreams at a frantic pace.

Escaping through the forest deep,
To the sorcerer's lair untold,
Where ancient secrets softly seep,
Into tales both brave and bold.

With each step, the magic grows,
Fairy lights twinkle like stars,
In the air, a sweetness flows,
As she dances without bars.

The sorcerer, with a knowing smile,
Awaits her in his hidden space,
Held captive by her lovely style,
In the hush of moonlit grace.

Together they weave fate's design,
With every twirl, enchantment spins,
In harmony, their hearts align,
As a new creation begins.

Secrets of the Mystic Petals

In a hush where silence sings,
Mystic petals softly gleam,
Cradling all that magic brings,
In the stillness, dreams redeem.

Underneath the ancient trees,
Stories whisper through the leaves,
Touched by soft and gentle breeze,
A promise that the heart believes.

Every color, every hue,
Holds a tale of realms unknown,
In secrets woven, pure and true,
A garden where love has grown.

Butterflies, in flight so free,
Carry echos through the air,
Bringing back the harmony,
Of a time when magics flare.

Feathers whispered in the bloom,
As starlight weaves the tapestry,
In this world of sweet perfume,
Lies the heart of mystery.

The Crib of Curious Wonders

In a nook where shadows play,
A crib of dreams in soft array.
Toys that whisper tales untold,
Of magic lands and treasures gold.

Beneath the watch of silver stars,
A lullaby from distant bars.
Each note a key to dreams that gleam,
Awakening the heart to dream.

The night unfolds its velvet shroud,
As moonbeams dance and laugh aloud.
Each twinkle sparks a tale anew,
Where endless wonders come in view.

Soft pillows stitched with twinkling thread,
Embrace the thoughts that gently spread.
As whispers wind through slumber's gate,
Curious wonders softly wait.

So close your eyes and breathe in deep,
For in this crib, the secrets sleep.
With every sigh and dream's soft flutter,
Awaits the joy of quiet utter.

Mystical Whirls of Gossamer Light

In twilight's embrace, shadows entwine,
Gossamer threads of magic shine.
Spinning round in a waltz so bright,
Mystical whirls of soft, pure light.

They dance like whispers on a breeze,
Through ancient woods and timeless trees.
Carrying dreams on wings so free,
Glimmers bright as the stars we see.

With every flicker, stories weave,
Of realms beyond, where hearts believe.
In this embrace of night's delight,
We find our path in the glowing sight.

The air is thick with sparkles rare,
A tapestry of magic's dare.
Each twirl unveils a fearless flight,
In the mystical whirls of light.

So let your spirit take to the skies,
And follow where the starlight lies.
In dreams, we'll dance, our hearts in sight,
Through ethereal realms of shimmering light.

Beneath the Canopy of Spells

In a grove where silence dwells,
Whispers float beneath the spells.
Tales of old in shadows blend,
Where time and magic gently bend.

The leaves, they shimmer with mystique,
Guarding secrets words can't speak.
Beneath the arch of nature's grace,
We find enchantment in this place.

A chorus hums, a hidden tune,
Bathe in the glow of silver moon.
Each flicker holds a promise dear,
That truth resides when hearts draw near.

With every step, the light unfolds,
A labyrinth of dreams in golds.
In shadows deep, our spirits swell,
Beneath the canopy of spells.

So wander forth with open mind,
In these woods, your fate you'll find.
For love and magic, side by side,
Guide us through the evening tide.

The Elixir of Twilight's Sighs

As daylight fades and whispers sigh,
Beneath the stretch of twilight sky.
An elixir brews, a potion rare,
Filled with secrets of the air.

Fleeting moments, softly caught,
In every drop, a lesson taught.
Brewed with laughter, tears anew,
A blend of all that we've been through.

Stirred with hope and dreams aglow,
This sacred mix, it starts to flow.
Sip gently on the evening light,
In twilight's arms, all feels just right.

With every taste, the heart will soar,
To realms where love is evermore.
The essence sweet, it draws us near,
To magic held in twilight's tear.

So gather 'round and share the bliss,
In this elixir, find your kiss.
With twilight's sighs, the world will shift,
Awakening the souls adrift.

Twilight Secrets Among the Blossoms

As the sun dips low in the sky,
Whispers of twilight start to sigh.
Petals glisten, dew-kissed fair,
Secrets linger in the air.

Shadows dance on the garden's floor,
Dreams awaken, glimpses of lore.
Crickets serenade the dusk's embrace,
Time stands still in this sacred space.

The moon ascends with a gentle grace,
Illuminating each hidden place.
Stars emerge in a celestial sea,
Every bloom holds a mystery.

Beneath the boughs where magic grows,
In the silence, enchantment flows.
Heartbeats sync with the night's soft song,
Here in the twilight, we all belong.

With every breath, the secrets weave,
A tapestry that none can leave.
These blossoms carry tales untold,
In their beauty, the night unfolds.

The Garden of Infinite Wishes

In a garden where wishes bloom,
Hope lifts its fragile plume.
Every flower, a wish to share,
Spinning dreams in the gentle air.

Petals of gold and silver dew,
Guard precious secrets like the new.
Whispers float on the breeze so light,
Carrying dreams into the night.

Glowing lanterns sway in the trees,
Entwined with laughter and honeyed breeze.
A wish upon every star, so bright,
Guides the heart toward its delight.

Each heartbeat sows a blossom anew,
In the soil where hopes pursue.
Every ray of sunlight's spark,
Sows the seeds of dreams in the dark.

As shadows dance and the day can't stay,
Wishes take flight, come what may.
The garden whispers, soft and clear,
In this haven, all wishes adhere.

Fragrant Echoes of Imagination

In the forest where fragrances twine,
Imagination starts to shine.
Each scent unfolds a tale, a spark,
Guiding wanderers through the dark.

Lilacs whisper of love from afar,
While wild roses absorb the star.
Echoes linger in the fragrant breeze,
Memories woven like dappled leaves.

Moss cushions secrets, ancient and wise,
Among the roots, where magic lies.
The air shimmers with colors bright,
Painting canvases of pure delight.

A canvas of scent to explore,
Each breath reveals an opened door.
Creativity flows like the river's song,
In the fragrant echoes, we belong.

As petals fall, they spark the mind,
Releasing wonders, deeply entwined.
In this enchanting, fragrant land,
Imagination blooms, plush and grand.

A Mystical Journey Through Petals

On a path where petals glisten,
Whispered dreams beg to be listened.
Each step taken is a tale untold,
A journey where hearts unfold.

Butterflies dance in the twilight mist,
Guiding souls with a gentle twist.
Every blossom a portal to roam,
In this garden, all spirits feel home.

Echoes of laughter, a tranquil tune,
Fill the air like a sweet monsoon.
Colors swirl in a vibrant sea,
A mystical dance, wild and free.

Through bramble and boughs, the magic weaves,
Every petal whispers, never leaves.
The moonlight bathes the journey's grace,
In nature's arms, we find our place.

As dawn breaks softly, dreams dissolve,
Yet the petals' magic will evolve.
In every journey's fleeting breath,
Life's petals share their dance of death.

Blooming Secrets in the Hearth's Glow

In the heart's warm light, they gleam,
Whispers of hope that softly beam,
Petals unfurling, truth in bloom,
Dreams take flight, dispelling gloom.

Magic stirs in every hue,
Bright as the morning, fresh as dew,
Stories circle like the flame,
Each one kissed with love's own name.

Secrets dance in the flickering fire,
Embers spark a deep desire,
From shadows rise, old tales retold,
In the hearth, their warmth unfolds.

With a gentle sigh, they sway,
In the glow of the end of day,
Binding hearts with silken threads,
In a tapestry that love spreads.

Enchanted nights, so rich and rare,
Hold the secrets that we share,
Blooming softly in the dark,
Carried softly by a lark.

Sorcery in the Sweetest Fragrance

Amidst the blooms, a spell is cast,
Where memories linger, shadows past,
Lavender dances on the breeze,
Whispers of magic in the trees.

Rose petals fall like secrets shared,
Each gentle scent, a heart ensnared,
Lilies unfold with graceful art,
Filling the air, they touch the heart.

Minty coolness, fresh and bright,
Invokes the dreams of endless night,
Breezes carry tales from far,
Guided by an evening star.

A potion brews within the air,
Floral notes, beyond compare,
Moments weave, so sweet and sly,
In the garden, where night doth lie.

Beneath the cloak of twilight's kiss,
We find the magic we long miss,
In every scent, a story sings,
Of sorcery in nature's rings.

A Dance in the Whispering Thicket

In the thicket where shadows play,
The moonlight weaves a silver ray,
Branches sway, as if to prance,
Inviting all to join the dance.

Leaves rustle softly, secrets hum,
Nature's chorus, a beating drum,
Each little creature, in delight,
Joins the dance beneath the night.

Stars twinkle like a thousand eyes,
Watching over with gentle sighs,
As whispers rise from the cool ground,
Lost in magic, they swirl around.

With every step, the thicket glows,
A secret rhythm that ebbs and flows,
Spirits twirl in timeless grace,
In this enchanted, sacred space.

Hold your breath and take a chance,
Embrace the night, join in the dance,
Within this woods, where dreams are spun,
The thicket's magic has just begun.

Petals Unraveling from Arcane Hands

From ancient palms, the petals fall,
Whispers echo, a haunting call,
Each fragment tells a story dear,
Of love and loss, of hope and fear.

Arcane hands weave threads of fate,
In twilight's glow, they softly wait,
With every slip, a promise made,
In the garden where memories fade.

Crisp and fragile like morning light,
They beckon forth the tender night,
Spelled by hands both strong and kind,
Through the petals, dreams unwind.

Let them drift on gentle gales,
Carrying forth forgotten tales,
In every twist, a tale unfolds,
In whispered lore, their magic holds.

So heed the signs the night reveals,
Trust in the heart and what it feels,
For in each petal's soft embrace,
Lies the ancient, timeless grace.

A Spellbound Serenade

In twilight's glow where secrets lie,
The whispers weave, as shadows sigh.
With wand in hand and heart so bold,
A melody of magic unfolds.

Through ancient woods where fairies play,
The spellbound notes begin to sway.
Each sound a charm, a sweet delight,
Enchanting dreams till morning light.

With every chord the stars align,
The air is thick with strands divine.
A harmony of hopes set free,
In this enchanted reverie.

Beneath the arch of willow's grace,
The evening hums, a soft embrace.
Each echo sings of love's true art,
A symphony that stirs the heart.

In moonlit hush, the night will hold,
A tale of magic yet untold.
So let the serenade take flight,
And weave its charm on dreams tonight.

The Child and the Celestial Petal

In a garden bright, where wonders grow,
A child, so sweet, with eyes aglow.
Finds a petal, soft and rare,
Whispering tales upon the air.

It dances lightly on a breeze,
Catching laughter, playful tease.
With every flutter, secrets share,
The magic held within its care.

The stars above begin to twinkle,
While dreams around the petals sprinkle.
A child's heart holds the purest light,
Guiding the petals through the night.

In twilight's arms, adventures bloom,
Across the sky, a gentle loom.
The petal glows with every tale,
While laughter rings like a silver veil.

Together they fly, the child and bloom,
Through a world where shadows loom.
For in their dance, the cosmos sways,
Creating magic through the days.

Enigma of the Dancing Flower

In a meadow lush, where dreams reside,
A flower twirls, with grace and pride.
Its petals swirl in colors bright,
A captivating, wondrous sight.

As evening falls and shadows creep,
The flower stirs from slumber deep.
With whispers soft, it starts to sway,
Unveiling secrets of the day.

It tells of journeys far and wide,
Of starlit paths, where spirits guide.
Each dance a story, every turn,
A flicker of magic that will burn.

Upon the breeze, a sweet perfume,
A promise held within its bloom.
With every sway, the night enthralls,
As moonlight casts its silver calls.

In harmony with all it knows,
The dancing flower gently glows.
A timeless riddle, pure and true,
A wondrous dance for me and you.

Whispers of Petal and Moon

In the hush of night, where shadows blend,
Two hearts converge, with dreams to send.
A petal falls, soft as a sigh,
Embracing hopes that touch the sky.

The moon above, a watchful eye,
Glistening paths where wishes lie.
Together they weave a tale so sweet,
Of love and light, where spirits meet.

With gentle rustle, the petal flutters,
Carrying secrets, as love mutters.
In quiet tones, their whispers flow,
As night unfolds, and stars aglow.

Through winding paths of silver streams,
The whispers dance within our dreams.
Bound by magic, forever near,
In every sigh, your voice I hear.

So here beneath the moon's soft gaze,
We paint our souls in starlit blaze.
With every petal, love resumes,
In whispers shared, our hearts find rooms.

Tales Beneath the Starlit Canopy

In whispered night, the stories gleam,
The starlit skies weave secrets, it seems.
With shadows dancing on the grass,
Each twinkle sparks a tale to pass.

The owls hoot softly, their wisdom vast,
The moonlight's glow through branches cast.
A shimmering brook hums a gentle tune,
As whispers echo beneath the moon.

Fireflies flicker like scattered dreams,
In this enchanted space, nothing is as it seems.
Each rustle and sigh holds a lingering lore,
Around the trees, spirits soar and explore.

Beneath the boughs where lost tales reside,
Wanderers seek what the heart can't hide.
In starlit scribbles, fate weaves its plot,
In the silence of night, every moment is caught.

So come, dear traveler, lay down your doubts,
Amidst the magic, let your soul shout.
For every starlit night holds a special grace,
In the secrets of the dark, find your rightful place.

Wandering Spirits of the Garden

In the garden's hush, whispers take flight,
Where shadows and blossoms unite in the night.
Each petal a canvas, soft stories unfurl,
As spirits awaken, they dance and twirl.

Moonflower blooms with a silvery hue,
Telling tales of the dreams that are pure and true.
The daisies nod gently, keeping their watch,
While the pathways of starlight begin to notch.

Beneath the old willow, secrets unfold,
In rustling leaves, the ancients are told.
Every bud holds the echoes of lore,
In silence they whisper, in shadows they soar.

Crickets play symphonies, soft and serene,
As night wraps the garden in emerald green.
The wanderers linger, touched by the breeze,
Finding solace in whispers, finding ease.

So tread softly here, where the spirits abide,
Among blooms of wonder, let your heart glide.
For in this realm, magic dances and sways,
In the wandering garden, where twilight stays.

The Allure of the Midnight Bloom

In the hush of night when the secrets sigh,
Emerging blooms reach to the velvet sky.
Their petals glisten, kissed by the dew,
Mysteries deepen in shades of midnight blue.

Bathed in silver, the blossoms awake,
With a fragrance that swirls like the dawn's gentle break.
Each bud unfurls as if to confess,
The beauty of night, a singular bless.

A soft breeze whispers through velvet leaves,
Carrying dreams that the night retrieves.
In the heart of darkness, beauty ignites,
Wrapping the world in soft, twinkling lights.

The moon, a guardian, watches with care,
As shadows dance lightly through the cool night air.
Each bloom a secret, each star a guide,
In the garden of night, where magic does bide.

So linger awhile under night's gentle embrace,
Where every midnight bloom takes its place.
For in this sacred moment, souls intertwine,
In the allure of the night, forever divine.

A Ballet of Petals and Stars

In twilight's glow, where light begins to fade,
A ballet unfolds as the stars serenade.
Petals pirouette in the soft evening air,
A waltz of colors, tender and rare.

The daisies twirl with a charming delight,
While hyacinths sway in the silver light.
Together they dance upon whispers of breeze,
Creating a symphony of floral ease.

Night sinks deep, draping soft shades of blue,
As shadows and starlight unveil something new.
With each gentle step, the world holds its breath,
In this fragrant ballet, there's life and there's death.

The cosmos joins in with a glimmering show,
Every twinkling star feels the ebb and the flow.
From the hush of the garden, beauty takes flight,
In a magnificent dance under the moonlight.

So come, take my hand, let the petals inspire,
As the garden ignites with a gentle desire.
For in this grand ballet where dreams softly swirl,
Magic and starlight forever unfurl.

Moonlit Dances in a Mystical Realm

In silver light, the shadows sway,
Beneath the whispering trees they play.
Glimmers twinkle on the brook,
Where ancient secrets dare to look.

Fairies twirl with silken grace,
In every heart, a hidden place.
The moon bestows its gentle gleam,
We dance beneath a silver dream.

With laughter spun from essences sweet,
We conjure worlds where wonders meet.
In luminescent fields we roam,
In this enchanted, fleeting home.

The night unfolds its starry thread,
While dreams and whispers softly spread.
Together we shall weave our fate,
In rhythms shared, we celebrate.

As dawn approaches, colors bloom,
But in our hearts, no trace of gloom.
For every dance beneath the moon,
Shall echo in our hearts, a tune.

Fragrant Journeys Beyond the Stars

On fragrant winds, the night unfolds,
With stories whispered, softly told.
Through galaxies, we drift afar,
Chasing dreams where wishes are.

With each new scent, a memory glows,
Of starlit paths where time flows.
In gardens rich with cosmic cheer,
We gather treasures, far and near.

Among the blossoms, laughter sings,
In realms of hope, imaginings.
With petals bright, we chart our course,
Guided by love's eternal force.

Through cosmic doors, we find our way,
In shimmering hues of dusk and day.
The nectar sweet, the journey bold,
In fragrant tales, our hearts unfold.

So let us wander, hand in hand,
Across the vast, enchanted land.
Beyond the stars, our spirits soar,
In fragrant dreams, forevermore.

The Enchanted Child's Play

In meadows bright where wildflowers grow,
Children dance with hearts aglow.
With laughter soft as morning light,
They weave enchantments, pure delight.

Through hidden woods, they skip and twirl,
Each secret path, a magic swirl.
With sticks for wands, they cast their spells,
And every nook, a story dwells.

In the hush of twilight's tender grace,
They chase the stars, a wondrous race.
With moonbeams caught in playful hands,
They dream of far-off, mythical lands.

With whispers sweet, they speak to trees,
And dance to tune of gentle breeze.
In every shadow, a friend is found,
In laughter's song, their joy unbound.

Let the world fade, let the magic play,
In every heart, a child will stay.
In moments bright, forever stay,
In the heart of every child's play.

Petals of Time and Space

In gardens vast where petals bloom,
Lay whispers borne from ancient loom.
Each flower holds a tale to tell,
Of time's embrace, a whispered spell.

As seasons dance, the colors change,
In patterns rich, sometimes strange.
With every petal that drifts away,
Time unfurls, night meets day.

The scent of jasmine fills the air,
A fleeting moment, soft and rare.
In every breath, a memory lives,
A gift from earth that nature gives.

In twilight's realm, the stars ignite,
A cosmic dance, a wondrous sight.
With every wish upon the breeze,
We gather hope among the trees.

So time may pass and space may bend,
But in our hearts, the magic blends.
With petals soft, our stories trace,
The endless weave of time and space.

A Carousel of Dreams in the Grove

In the grove where shadows dance,
Whispers secrets of a chance.
Leaves that twirl in playful shrieks,
Telling tales that nature speaks.

Beneath the boughs, a dream takes flight,
Spinning softly in the light.
Glimmers glisten, soft and bright,
Guiding hearts through endless night.

Carousel of wishes spun,
Round and round, till day is done.
Magic weaves through every sigh,
In the grove where dreams can fly.

Lanterns glow like stars at play,
Leading lost ones on their way.
Every corner holds a spark,
Filling hearts with warmth from dark.

So come and ride this wondrous wheel,
Feel the joy, the magic real.
In this grove, let spirits soar,
Carousel of dreams, evermore.

Riddles Linger in the Floral Depths

Among the blooms, a riddle stirs,
Softly whispered, nature purrs.
Petals weave their mysteries tight,
Fragrant secrets float in light.

Beneath the surface, answers hide,
In every color, dreams abide.
Can you solve the tales they tell?
In the garden, all is well.

Fluttering wings and buzzing hums,
Echo answers, nature comes.
In the depths where flowers bloom,
Wisdom rises, dispelling gloom.

Follow the paths where shadows blend,
Trust the rumors that they send.
In this theater of pure delight,
Riddles linger, day and night.

So ponder deep, let wonders flow,
In the garden where secrets grow.
Every petal, a tale to keep,
Riddles linger in conversation's sweep.

Echoes of Spells among the Greenery

In the forest, whispers weave,
Echoed spells that none believe.
Hushed enchantments on the breeze,
Linger softly in the trees.

Shadows shift with ancient grace,
Every root holds time and space.
Mystic forces pulse alive,
In this grove, where dreams arrive.

Notes of magic swirl and twine,
Cloaked in green, where hearts entwine.
Echoes fill the air with song,
Binding nature, fierce and strong.

Beneath the canopy, they play,
Guarding secrets night and day.
Listen close, and you shall hear,
Echoed spells that draw you near.

So wander through this verdant maze,
Feel the magic, hear the praise.
Among the greenery so pure,
Echoes of spells forever lure.

The Blooms that Speak in Silken Hues

In the garden where colors clash,
Blooms that speak with every flash.
Silken petals, soft and bright,
Whisper grace in morning light.

Voices weave through fragrant air,
Sharing stories, wild and rare.
Every blossom sings its tune,
Underneath the watchful moon.

Listen close to floral sighs,
In their song, the spirit flies.
Vibrant hues that catch the eye,
Tell of moments that don't die.

Each arrangement holds a dream,
Colors blend and softly gleam.
In this world where blooms unite,
Sorrow fades and hearts take flight.

So wander forth among the blooms,
Feel their magic in the rooms.
In these silken hues, find peace,
Where every whisper brings release.

Moonshadow in Bloom

Beneath the silvered sky's embrace,
The flowers dance, a tender grace.
Each petal glows with whispered dreams,
In moonlight's hush, their magic beams.

They sway with secrets, soft and bright,
While shadows play, the world ignites.
A symphony of night unfolds,
Where stories weave and hearts grow bold.

In twilight's glow, time stands still,
The garden breathes, a gentle thrill.
With every breeze, a tale anew,
In moonshadowed paths, hopes renew.

The starlit blooms, they softly call,
To those who wander, lest they fall.
In every hue, a journey starts,
A dance of dreams within our hearts.

Each night so full, yet fleeting fast,
A reminder of the shadows cast.
In blooms of gold and dusk's perfume,
We find our way, in moonshadow's bloom.

The Radiance of Childlike Wonder

In a world where fairies take their flight,
And stars spill dreams with pure delight.
With laughter bright, the skies ignite,
Childlike wonder, forever light.

With every step, a tale unfolds,
In shimmering glades and glinting golds.
A twinkling spark in every eye,
Where magic lives and spirits fly.

The whispers of the woods resound,
Where laughter echoes all around.
With every turn, a new surprise,
The beauty seen through youthful eyes.

The breeze carries secrets of the day,
In playful tunes, they gently sway.
With open hearts, we dare to roam,
In dreams, we find our heart's true home.

Each fleeting moment, bright and clear,
The essence of our childhood near.
In glowing memories, we'll hover,
In the radiance of childlike wonder.

So let us dance beneath the moon,
And chase the sun, for morning's boon.
In every laughter, sweet and pure,
In childlike dreams, our hearts endure.

A Garden's Heartbeat

In every bloom, a story lies,
A heartbeat felt 'neath sunny skies.
Amongst the petals, whispers grow,
A garden's life, a gentle flow.

The rustling leaves sing soft and low,
As dew-kissed morn begins to glow.
Each bud a promise, fresh and new,
In vibrant colors, life shines through.

With every breath, the garden sighs,
In fragrant hues of summer skies.
A waltz of nature, pure and sweet,
A dance of life, where hearts will meet.

From roots to blooms, the cycle spins,
In harmony, the magic wins.
With whispers soft, the petals sway,
In a garden's heart, there's always play.

A tapestry of life unfolds,
In daylight's warmth and evening's golds.
With open arms, the world we greet,
In every heartbeat, love's retreat.

So here we stand, amidst the grace,
In nature's arms, we find our place.
In each petal's touch, each gentle beat,
A garden's heart, forever sweet.

The Memory of Whispering Flowers

In twilight's hush, the flowers speak,
Their petals brush with secrets meek.
A fragrant breeze, the softest sigh,
In memories of blooms that never die.

Each blossom tells a tale unknown,
Of whispered dreams and seeds that've grown.
Their colors fade, yet love remains,
In garden paths, where hope sustains.

With gentle rustle, stories weave,
In every leaf, a world achieved.
The past and present intertwined,
In each embrace, a truth defined.

The sun dips low, and shadows play,
As twilight dances, dreams relay.
With every petal, a soul's delight,
In memory's arms, we find the light.

So cherish blooms and every glance,
In their soft whispers, find your chance.
For in the heart, the flowers grow,
With every sigh, their love will flow.

The garden holds the echoes near,
In colors bright that disappear.
A reminder of what once was ours,
In the memory of whispering flowers.

A Tapestry of Elysian Fragrances

In garden's heart, the roses bloom,
Their petals whisper of sweet perfume.
Beneath the shade where the lilies sway,
Fragrant dreams softly drift away.

Dew-kissed herbs in the morning light,
Basil, mint, unfolding delight.
A symphony of scents in the breeze,
Nature's gift, our senses seize.

Lavender dances in twilight's embrace,
Iridescent thoughts in a lavender space.
Hints of jasmine on a moonlit ride,
Cradled in night where the secrets hide.

With each soft sigh, the petals sigh,
Opening wide to the amber sky.
Their stories weave through night's gentle shroud,
A tapestry bright, both tender and loud.

Inhale the world, in each fragrant thread,
A fleeting moment, where whispers spread.
Elysian fragrances, a gift to bestow,
In the garden of dreams, forever to grow.

Shadows of the Fairy's Playground

In twilight's glow, where whispers blend,
Shadows weave and the dreams extend.
Tiny lanterns flicker bright,
Guiding footsteps through the night.

Mischievous sprites in their dance of delight,
Play with shadows, taking flight.
They twirl and spin in a world so fair,
Crafting magic in the cool night air.

Lost in laughter, the echoes abound,
While the moonlight drapes o'er the ground.
A symphony of twinkles, gleeful and sly,
Crafting mischief beneath starry sky.

Violets bloom in enchanted glades,
Where secrets sleep in the darkened shades.
Everglade paths where the wild things roam,
In shadows, all find a place called home.

So linger awhile 'neath the moon's soft gleam,
In the fairy's playground, dwell in a dream.
For the heart knows joy when the shadows play,
In the realm of magic, forever stay.

The Secret Life of Flora

In a quiet corner of the garden's heart,
Flora's secrets play their part.
Petals flutter in whispered tone,
In nature's chorus, they're never alone.

Roots entwined in soil so deep,
Where ancient wisdom quietly sleeps.
Each sprout and leaf, a tale to tell,
Of sunlit mornings and soft-night swell.

Butterflies dance, a ballet sublime,
With every flutter, they keep perfect time.
Pollinators hum their magical song,
In unseen worlds where they belong.

Frost-kissed mornings, painted anew,
Secrets awaken in every hue.
A bloom's gentle sigh, a fragrant muse,
In the sunlight's warmth, it's life they choose.

Beneath the stars, their stories entwine,
The silent whispers of flora divine.
In every petal, each vibrant sigh,
Lives the secret life where mysteries lie.

Where Dreams Take Root

In the meadow's cradle, where dreams take root,
Gentle whispers from a distant flute.
A tapestry spun of silken threads,
Where wishes bloom and fantasy spreads.

Clouds drift softly in a cerulean sea,
Carrying hopes of what could be.
Each blade of grass sways with a tune,
Under the watchful eye of the moon.

Sparkling stars weave a silver line,
Guiding dreams with their gentle shine.
Each breath of wind, a promise unfurled,
A pathway to magic in a sleeping world.

In the heart of the night, where shadows gleam,
Lies the sanctuary of every dream.
A place where thoughts and wishes collide,
In the meadow's embrace, where dreams abide.

So close your eyes, let the visions bloom,
In the garden of dreams, release the gloom.
For in this haven, where love can sprout,
Dreams take root, casting shadows out.

The Celestial Dance of Petals

In twilight's glow, the petals sway,
Dancing dreams in soft array.
Stars above, they weave and twine,
In the night, their colors shine.

Whispers of the moonlit breeze,
Guide the blossoms with such ease.
Each flutter brings a tale anew,
In this garden, magic grew.

Candles flicker, shadows play,
Time suspended, night and day.
Every turn a secret spun,
Under the gaze of the silver sun.

Petals drift on silken air,
Carrying wishes, free and fair.
With each fall, a wish takes flight,
Chasing dreams into the night.

In the dance, what wonders wait,
Fates entwined, a twist of fate.
Nature's rhythm beats so sweet,
In this realm, our hearts do meet.

Ascendancy of the Enchanted Blossom

From humble roots, the blossom grows,
Amidst the thorns, a beauty shows.
In vibrant hues, it greets the light,
A symbol of hope, shining bright.

With every dawn, new life awakes,
The world transformed by what it makes.
Each petal whispers, soft and low,
Of ancient tales that ebb and flow.

An enchanted breeze weaves through the trees,
A lullaby sung by buzzing bees.
The air saturated with sweet delight,
In this sacred space, hearts take flight.

And as the sun begins to set,
The garden holds no room for regret.
For every bloom, a story told,
Of love and magic, brave and bold.

In twilight's breath, a promise forms,
In shadows where the spirit warms.
The blossom's reign, a sight to see,
In its glow, we are truly free.

Symphony of the Mystical Garden

Listen close, the garden sings,
With every bloom, the magic clings.
A symphony beneath the stars,
Echoes of joy from near and far.

Petals twirl in a vibrant spree,
Nature's song, a wild decree.
Fleeting moments caught in time,
Crafting rhythms, sweet as rhyme.

Leaves rustle, a gentle cheer,
Whispers echo for all to hear.
Fragrant scents weave through the air,
A tapestry beyond compare.

Every color, a note sublime,
Painting silence with the chime.
In harmony, the spirits dance,
In this garden, lost in trance.

As dusk descends, the stars arise,
Winking down from velvet skies.
The symphony of life unfolds,
In this realm, the heart beholds.

And as the night begins to fade,
The garden sleeps, a dream is laid.
Tomorrow's light will bring anew,
The symphony that sings for you.

Lovesongs in Petal Form

In every petal lies a tale,
A lovesong wrought, gentle and frail.
Whispers of longing through the air,
In fragrant notes, soft and rare.

Each blossom knows the heart's desire,
Igniting dreams like a secret fire.
Colors blend, a palette bright,
Two souls entwined beneath the light.

With every breeze, sweet echoes play,
Carried forth as night turns day.
A serenade of love's embrace,
In nature's arms, we find our place.

Petals fall like whispers sweet,
A memory shared in a heartbeat.
In the garden, hopes take flight,
Beneath the glow of silver light.

So let the blossoms sing their song,
A tapestry where we belong.
In every petal, magic swirls,
A lovesong shared between two worlds.

Tomorrow's bloom will tell the tale,
Of love that shines, will never fail.
In the garden, forevermore,
Lovesongs echo, an endless lore.

www.ingramcontent.com/pod-product-compliance
Ingram Content Group UK Ltd.
Pitfield, Milton Keynes, MK11 3LW, UK
UKHW021510280125
4335UKWH00035B/775